D0090339

Fidelity

Fidelity

GRACE PALEY

Farrar, Straus and Giroux

New York

Farrar, Straus and Giroux

18 West 18th Street, New York 10011

Distributed in Canada by Douglas & McIntyre Ltd.

Printed in the United States of America

First edition, 2008

Library of Congress Cataloging-in-Publication Data

Paley, Grace.

   Fidelity / Grace Paley.— 1st ed.

     p.   cm.

   ISBN-13: 978-0-374-29906-4 (hardcover : alk. paper)

   ISBN-10: 0-374-29906-4 (hardcover : alk. paper)

   I. Title.

 PS3566.A46F53 2008

 811'54—dc22

                        2007045747

Designed by Dorothy Schmiderer Baker

www.fsgbooks.com

10   9   8   7   6   5   4   3   2

To Nora, Danny, and my grandchildren

CONTENTS

•

•

PROVERBS

A person's anger should be respected
even when it isn't shared

a person's happiness should be shared
even if it isn't understood

a person should be understood   though
he has brought both his brows together
in anger and also suddenly begun to laugh

a person should be in love most of
the time   this is the last proverb
and may be learned by all the organs
capable of bodily response

ANTI-LOVE POEM

Sometimes you don't want to love the person you love
you turn your face away from that face
whose eyes lips might make you give up anger
forget insult   steal sadness of not wanting
to love   turn away then turn away   at breakfast
in the evening   don't lift your eyes from the paper
to see that face in all its seriousness   a
sweetness of concentration   he holds his book
in his hand   the hard-knuckled winter wood-
scarred fingers   turn away   that's all you can
do   old as you are to save yourself   from love

ON OCCASION

I forget the names of my friends
and the names of the flowers in
my garden   my friends remind me
Grace   it's us   the flowers just
stand there stunned by the sun

A long time ago my mother said
darling   there are also wildflowers
but look   these I planted

my flowers are   pink and rose and
orange   they're sturdy   they make
new petals every day to fill in
their fat round faces

suddenly before thought I
called out ZINNIA   zinnia
zinnia   along came a sunny
        summer breeze   they swayed
        lightly bowed   I said   Mother

FATHERS

Fathers are
more fathering
these days   they have
accomplished this by
being more mothering

what luck for them that
women's lib happened   then
the dream of new fathering
began to shine in the eyes
of free women and was
irresistible

on the New York subways
and the mass transits
of other cities   one may
see fatherings of many colors
with their round babies on
their laps   this may also
happen in the countryside

these scenes were brand new
exciting for an old woman who
had watched the old fathers
gathering once again in

familiar army camps and com-
fortable war rooms to consider
the necessary eradication of
the new fathering fathers
(who are their sons) as well
as the women and children who
will surely be in the way

why shouldn't men look at women
and women look at men
and women look at women
and men look at men
why shouldn't they
size each other up (as
we used to say)

why isn't there more
of that looking   that
casual catching of
breath in plain
appreciation or rejection   why
isn't there more of it   what
old people sometimes ex-
perienced   as shock and a
dangerous heartbeat which
sometimes erupted into
love at first sight (as
it is called to this day)
and as old people we must
warn   it may once in a startling
while last forever (as it
is called)

I MET A WOMAN ON THE PLANE

she came from somewhere around Tampa
she was going to Chicago
I liked her a lot
she'd had five children
no she'd had six   one died
at twenty-three days

people said   at least you didn't
get too attached

she had married at sixteen   she
married again twenty years later
she said she loved her first husband
just couldn't manage life

five small children? I said
no not that
   what?   him?
no   me she said
I couldn't get over that baby girl
everyone else did   the big
kids   you'll drive us all crazy
they said   but that baby   you can't
believe her beautifulness
when I came into the kids' room

in her little crib   not a month old
not breathing   they say get over it
it's more than ten years   go away   leave
us for a while   so I did that   here I am she said
where are you going

you can't think without thinking about something
my friends who are Buddhists are sometimes thinking
weeks on end about how to think about nothing
they are often successful
                              sometimes looking
at that famous sculpture (or a picture of it)
I think   oh he is surely not thinking about any-
thing   he only wants to give the appearance to
passersby for some reason   or he needs to hold
his heavy head in his hands which will allow
thoughts or ideas into his stoniness
                                  just as I   putting
my pen to paper am pretty sure that something
which has pressed upon my breath beyond bearing
will appear in words   take shape and singing
let me go on with my life

T H E N

when she came to meet him at the ferry
he said   you are so pale   worn   so
frail   standing on her toes
to reach his ear   she whispered
I am an old woman   oh then
he was always kind

freedom has overtaken me   I
had run ahead of it for years
along an interesting but
narrow road   obeyed at least
half the rules imposed by
lovers children   a house a
political position   now out
of breath probably   I'm stuck
freedom has hold of my jacket
won't let go   I am alone

before I was nobody
I was me   after
I was nobody   I
was me   I wish
I could have rested
in me a little longer
there was something
I was supposed to tell
but   it isn't allowed

a new york city man is
standing on the street corner
he's smiling up at a fireman hanging
on to the ladder of his fire engine

the fire engine passes between us
slowly it turns the corner   it is
going home to its firehouse

I am in a taxi stuck in traffic
I smile at the smiling man   he
nods his head courteously   we
know each other   our newyorkness

Thank God there is no god
or we'd all be lost

if it is He who sends us howling
in murderous despair   at torture
hatred   three or four times a generation
there'd be no hope   and if He permitted
peace to appear   then one day   great plates
of stone beneath the orchards and sea may
move slowly against one another   earthquake

if it is He who built that narrow a bridge
across which we are invited to walk
without fear while all around us
the old the lame the awkward the jumping-
up-and-down children are tumbling off
or sometimes pushed into the hideous
gorge   if it is He then we are surely lost

if it is He who offers free will but
only sometimes   a peculiar gift
for a people who have just distinguished
their right hand from their left

but if we are responsible con-
sider our frequent love for one another
because this is nowadays   we may be able
to look over great distances into
each other's eyes   these are the tele-
phonic electronic digital nowadays
famous for money and loneliness but we

have defeated Babel by accepting the words
of strangers in glorious translations   if

we can be responsible   if we have
become responsible

THE HARD-HEARTED RICH

Oh how hard the hard-hearted rich are
when they meet a working person in their places
of work   a cab or a restaurant kitchen
and the hard heart   beats and eases   the mouth
into saying well they do get minimum wage
probably and when they meet   an
ordinary bum or maybe a homeless person
on their street or broad boulevard
standing on the pavement common to
all the good shops   holding a paper cup or cap
asking for change   oh say the hard-hearted rich
they will use it for drugs or drink and be found
at midnight in drunken sleep in the doorway
of one of the best shops of all
Then the hard-hearted rich and
there are many many in our city
just as there are many many women and
men working in hard-driven poverty
or not working at all   oh the hard-hearted rich
move into the glorious evening of drinking and talking
and eating and drinking   again   into sleep
in their queen-size beds as though they
were queens with kings beside each other
and it's night and the moon's bright
light falls through the huge windows

then they decide to try
love   as a kind   of heart softener
they are tired and think to try   love

THEIR HONEST PURPOSE MOCKED

Or the past? I asked   you mean
going back to old diaries
notebooks full of me?   no   see how
the unusual earth is
wrapped around with forests
fields   the raging sea that is
trying to get away from us leaping
leaping falling to the shore
again and again   planted with stones
and with land mines   that explode
the little legs   of little children
I know I have gone too far   but
would go further if the poem
were not complete

What a terrible racket they made
beating all those swords into plowshares
people were deafened worldwide   letters
of protest   as well as serious essays
pointing out in the sensible way
of ordinary people   we no longer
use plowshares   swords have been
for generations the playthings
of boys and men

now the government that year happened
to be a poet   it explained
in a kindly way   citizens we had
in mind a living performing metaphor
using familiar religious themes and
literary memories   of course once we
get those useless plowshares there
may be a couple of economic or
industrial uses   we will even be able
to beat them back into swords should swords
still be required by boys and men

~

She said
        every sentence is an accusation
and I thought
        she speaks well
that child has always known what to say about the world
she has a beautiful face a clear head and cosmic notions
        My god, I said
        you're right   that's the way it is
the world speaks to you nowadays
                        in accusations
it doesn't leave you alone for a minute
it thinks everything is your fault   the world is like that
No she said
        I wasn't talking about the world
        I was talking about you
Yes I said   that's it   that's just what I meant

Life is as risky
as it is branchy

treetop and twigtip
are only the beginning

then comes the westwind to lean
and the northwind to turn

then the sunshine implores
and up all of us go

we are like any
greengrowing machinery

riding the daylight route
to darkness

BIRTH OF A CHILD

there they go
        beginning life
                all over again

the world is a cowering
        coward of a place
                won't stand up

for itself   what
        do they have in mind
                creating hope

wrong anyway
        hope was always there
                fluttering

its little
        pockmarked flag
                why

be so grandiose
        just do something
                now and then

Sometimes now when I sleep alone
I get a whiff of myself
and wonder   all these years   is this
the odor familiar to you
if so did you really like it   doesn't
seem so nice   you're unusually non-
sweaty for such an active man   but slightly
sweet when I hug you   nowadays
(or you me)   or put my head on your
pillow in our bed   I know it's you
a delicate odor of woodsmoke   and I breathe
you in a little   not surprised
I remember you were always delicious

I MET A SEDUCER

One day a seducer met a seducer
now said one   what do we do
fly into each other's arms said
the other   ugh said one   they turned
stood back to back   one
looked over one's shoulder   smiled
shyly   other turned seconds
too late   made a lovelier
shy smile   oh my dear said other
my own dear   said one

HAVING DINNER

My friend said   why are you so up
I mean reality is a terrible down
look at the facts   right there in the pasta
you can see it   the plausible future boiled
once more in its own gas   the end   bad luck
for our time   bad luck for literature
our dear language back to planet pudding
Yes   it is a terrible down   they blame it
on that tree   that apple of all knowing
I would eat it again he said

AN OCCASIONAL SPEECH AT THE INTERFAITH THANKSGIVING GATHERING

Anyone who gets to be
eighty years old says thank you
to the One in charge then im-
mediately begins to complain   why
were these years such a historical
mess   why was my happiness
and willing gratitude interfered with
every single decade   no sooner
were the normal spats with parents
lovers children ended than the
interfering greed of total strangers
probably eighty years old as well
and full of their own bloated thank-
fulness at unbelievable success in
the expropriation of what belonged
to other people and peoples not
to mention the economic degradation
leading to thanks engendering
profits in our own country and
in the innocent or colluding parts
of the world
                    I am sadly reminded
of the first couple of our American

thanksgivings   thank you   thank you
our first Americans together with
the Absolutely First Americans   within a gener-
ation or half of one the first Americans
proceeded to drive the Absolutely First
Americans from their villages   rivers
fields over mountains and across the con-
tinent   out out they cried almost at
the same time shouting thank you   thanks
                              thank you

IT DOESN'T MATTER IF

It doesn't matter if you were just born
or if you're dying
you have to sleep at night

then you wake up   the sun
insists no matter what
you turn even in sleep to light

all day will then furiously begin
your children will require bread
you may have to fight

to obtain it from the greedy owners of grain
who had learned how to grind it into gold
the old ones say there is food for everyone
wealth in the earth   but famine lies down
in its old green field   blight

in their last sleep the mothers moan
what of the child she must be fed
ah   in their ragged shrouds they hid
pocketfuls of ancient seed
inheritance against the coming night

TO THE VERMONT ARTS COUNCIL ON ITS FORTIETH BIRTHDAY

When I was forty   everything
was all right   it's true our children
with their ears to the pavement
were about to become that famous
city's generation   our neighborhood
noisy with their energetic global
intention   then in the very heart
of the prime of my life (as it was
called) the American War in Vietnam
(eight thousand miles away) entered
the newspapers

luckily artists and poets and
musicians were wide awake due to
their peculiar antennae   for instance
the poets on trucks   in churches had
already heard the voice of Vietnamese
children and the mural makers had seen
even before the photographers the
curious bombs like bouquets called
cluster   they painted the story that
the poets and musicians sang

as we say   that was then this is now
and we are here to congratulate
the Vermont Arts Council which
had the Vermont sense and aesthetic
energy to be born forty years ago
and finds itself as I did then
in the prime of life with another
American war with an unknown people
thousands of miles away luckily
Vermont the United States and the
Arts Council is deep in poets   most
of us with big mouths   (it is said)   even
                                    the gentlest

the very little girl looked at her grandfather
the way he was sprawled across his big wheelchair
his leg was crooked   it was bent the wrong way   she
watched his leg for two or three minutes   sometimes
it tried to move itself   it was interesting   she
gave him a Kleenex

then she wanted to see the important room   all
the women and men in a half circle of wheelchairs
looking straight at the television   some were
all right   many were hunched over   their heads
were twisted   that way they could see the tele-
vision better   sometimes people walked from
somewhere to someplace else right past the big
television faces   only one person yelled out
hey   you crazy   it was very interesting

on the way back to see her grandfather in
his window corner she stopped   a man she'd seen
last week was bobbing his head and waving his
arms and shouting go away and stop it and go
to hell   other   words   very loud   no one came
she watched him for about five minutes   then he
took a breath   he was quiet   she saw that he had
finished being interesting   bye-bye she said   she
waved   the man   exhausted softly said bye-bye

MY SISTER AND MY GRANDSON

I have been talking to my sister   she
may not know she's been dust and ashes
for the last two years   I talk to her
nearly every day

I've been telling her about our new baby
who is serious   comical   busy   dark   my
sister   out of all the rubble and grit
that is now her   my sister mutters   what
about our old baby   he was smart   loving
so beautiful

yes yes I said   listen   just last week
he stopped at my hallway door   he saw
your small Turkish rug   he stared at it
he fell to his knees his arms wide   crying
Jeannie   oh my own auntie Jeannie

remembered   ah   her hard whisper came to me
thank you Grace   now speak to him tell him
he's still my deepest love

FIDELITY

After supper I returned to
my reading book   I had
reached page one hundred
and forty   two hundred and twenty
more to go I had been thinking that
evening   as we spoke
early at dinner with a couple of young
people   of the dense improbable
life of that book in which I had become so comfortable
the characters were now my troubled companions
I knew them   understood I could
reenter these lives without loss
so firm my habitation   I scanned the shelves
some books so dear to me   I had missed them
leaned forward to take the work into
my hands   I took a couple of deep breaths
thought about the acceleration of days
yes   I could reenter them but . . .
No   how could I desert that other whole life
those others in their city basements
Abandonment   How could I have allowed myself
even thought of a half hour's distraction
when life had pages   or decades to go
so much was about to happen to people
I already know and nearly loved

I INVITED

I invited my mother and father into my dream
which included a table   chairs   a record player
an early evening hospitality   my
friends say that their parents are always present
to pester the night with little pearls of acid advice
my parents are not like that

I wanted to see my mother and father
together   They appeared   they organized their bodies
slowly they saw each other before they were
aware of me   She looked at him   my god   Zenya
how old you've grown in these forty years she said
also much shorter   is it true you never married?
my father was embarrassed   he was probably ashamed
to have outlived her   by so many years
What could they say?   then thank goodness they
remembered their own children
Well of course   he said   You knew the first little one
at least you gave her some pretty tight hugs
and kissed her from head to toe   The other one my son
a good man he worries
about my health   he asks me   do you have a fever
are you still coughing?   he was a doctor too
he lived long

                    my mother was amazed

my father says why not   It's common in this country
even I with a vicious heart attack lived to be eighty-nine
my mother says   my god   eighty-nine?
all those years did you think   of me?
all the time   he said   at my eightieth birthday I
told everybody I owe everything to you
that was very nice she said   reaching out
you were working so hard I didn't think you remembered me
from one day to the next

ॐ

  my lungs Catherine says he smoked
you know in bed for years till women's lib
came along said he couldn't do it anymore
it was too late for me the bastard he

killed me then there was Joan she
whispered Parkinson's me too Ellie said
me too they were OK used walkers
couldn't type though hard for old writers
a couple of tough double pneumonias long
recoveries
    we have one another now and then
a peculiar illness crops up we run like
real americans to computers and know
the diagnosis before the doctor my own
illness was headlined in the Times for
some reason I was proud the last time
my name appeared in the paper it was
with a friend years ago in jail during
the Vietnam war and I was only middle-aged

NEWS

although we would prefer to talk
and talk it into psychological the-
ory the prevalence of small genocides
or the recent disease floating
toward us from another continent we
must not   while she speaks her eyes
frighten us   she is only one person
she tells us her terrible news   we
want to leave the room we may not
we must listen   in this wrong world this
is what   we must do   we must bear it

W H O

the character in the dream speaks
I would never have invited him
he speaks again   he wants
to run things   I don't even know him

the second night   I think   maybe
I saw him about sixty years ago
he says   OK OK   he still
wants to run things

the third night   I say I'm tired
he says he's in charge   come on let's move it
I say   oh well . . .

the fourth night   I wake up
I've recognized him   I
know you   you've had your chance

he says   It's too late   I'm here

BRAVERY ON TENTH STREET

This morning   a man
his head hanging from
the weak curved stem
of neck   feeble wife
beside him   her hands
grip a walker   a small
shopping bag   knotted
to her wrist   she leans
slides toward him   he
turns his head   pain   looks
up   around   alarmed steadies
her   she is upright   they
walk ten or twelve steps
are suddenly stalled
she begins to drift   tremble
he stands   a twisted bulwark
his eyes on the pavement how
to get home   half a block
away   was life this long?

M A N Y

The reproductive
and recreational organs
of many of my older friends have
been declared redundant   dangerous
to the hardworking body

still after extreme surgeries
many of us in the pharmaceutical
west are able to live well   not
to be arrogant is essential

I have experienced the amputation
of my left breast   I hate its absence
but I'm at the door of a large noisy room
full of familiar faces   many
of us will not live long years   many
paying rigorous dues think we will

I needed to talk to my sister
talk to her on the telephone   I mean
just as I used to every morning
in the evening too whenever the
grandchildren said a sentence that
clasped both our hearts

I called   her phone rang four times
you can imagine my breath stopped   then
there was a terrible telephonic noise
a voice said   this number is no
longer in use   how wonderful I
thought   I can
call again they have not yet assigned
her number to another person despite
two years of absence due to death

SUDDENLY THERE'S POUGHKEEPSIE

what a hard time
the Hudson River has had
trying to get to the sea

it seemed easy enough to
rise out of Tear of
the Cloud and tumble
and run in little skips
and jumps   draining
        a swamp here and
    there   acquiring
streams and other smaller
rivers with similar
longings for the wide
imagined water

suddenly
there's Poughkeepsie
except for its spelling
an ordinary town but
the great heaving
ocean sixty miles away is
determined to reach
that town every day
and twice a day   in fact

drowning the Hudson River
in salt and mud
it is the moon's tidal
power over all the waters
of this earth at war with
gravity   the Hudson
perseveres   moving down
down   dignified
slower   look it has
become our Lordly Hudson
hardly flowing
          and we are
now in a poem by the poet
Paul Goodman   be quiet heart
home home
          then the sea

A CLOUD LIKE A TOWER

A cloud like a tower
nothing pillowy about it
Gaudi must have seen that
structure before descending
to Barcelona where
he raised his own with rounded
shoulders that
looked sharp   how?

I WENT OUT WALKING

My poems had gotten so heavy
I went out walking in
the springtime woods and I
carried a sack   a nice blue
string bag   with pen clipped in-
to the netting   also this
little notebook   and a wider
one for long line poems   my
eyeglasses   a comb   I thought
what if the late March wind
attacks my gray and tangled hair
       just then another poet
       crossed my path   his backpack
       already fat with poems and
       a pen in his teeth

some things are not
meant to be found
if you find them you
lose them again   if you
find them you lose them
don't look for them you
will only find them

believe me   I am
an unreliable
narrator   no story
I've ever told
was true   many people
have said this before
but they were lying

in autumn the leaves fall   high
on the hill   the rich man's
windows appear

NIGHT MORNING

To translate a poem
from thinking
into English
takes all night
night   nights and days

English does
the best it can   while
the mother's tongue   Russian
omits the verb to be
again and again and
is always interfering
with the excited in-
dustrious brain   wisely
the heart's beat asserts
control

also the newest English
argues with its old
singing ancestry
it thinks it knows best

finally   the night's
hard labor peers through
the morning window   observes

snow　birds　the sun caught
in white and black winter
birches　disentangles itself
addresses the ice-cold meadow
for hours on the beauty of
the color green

~

my heart leaps up when I behold
almost any valley or village in
the   embrace of US eighty-nine
from White River to Lake Champlain

I am less affected by rainbows   they are
handsome and fade into the damp sky
just ahead of the car

the children who are glad for
such beauty can now call out
look   look a rainbow   they never say

oh see the town   South Royalton
moving fast behind us   hugged
by the White River itself and
what about the splendid hills
of Sharon flattening into
hopeful farms   and then finally the drive
the drive downhill into our great city
Burlington   Lake Champlain rises up
before your eyes   then lies down to
accommodate the New York shore

I am with Wordsworth on most other
high perceptions   I must admit
to sharing his breathless hope
for a long life   still it is
too late   I am old already   that
prayer taken care of by health
and inheritance   still that long
curling highway made me think
of my leaping heart and then of
Wordsworth who with a couple
of other poets first taught
my heart to leap

ON THE PARK BENCH

she is telling the story to another woman
the woman is listening   she tells it again
the woman stops listening   there is another
woman   she tells her the story   she tells it
again   the woman walks away   why did she
do that?   the story is interesting   but it
must be heard three or four times   what
will she do?   she walks   she thinks she'll go home
she walks   she's tired   she sits down
on a bench under the old elm
a woman is waiting

THE IRISH POET

The Irish poet enters the hall late
as usual   no one is angry
several students have Yeats collections
on their laps   one student
waves a Patrick Kavanagh at him
he looks happy he says   ah

there are three teachers at the podium
they have been peering into
a computer full of poems which will be
flashed onto a screen   the poems
are by Shelley   Yeats   Bishop

they are serious teachers   these poems
are the early abysmal drafts
of great poets   the students are
encouraged   they have many abysmal
drafts themselves   they have usually
stopped at   oh   their second or
third draft   what if their longing
for their own true invention
of language is not strong enough   what
if they are satisfied too soon   there is
a long communal sigh at the screen full

of delicate poetic error   the Irish poet
smacks his head and sighs his own sigh
the students laugh and applaud

THE TELLING

I met a woman in the street   she
told me the whole story   I said
yes yes   then I told her the
whole story   she said unbelievable
then I turned the corner   there
was John   he said   but how did that
little family suddenly vanish
then walking walking we met
Elsa   she said what's wrong with
you two   you know the whole
story   first the boy   then him
then her   then that was that   but
they were just here John cried   on
Seventh Avenue standing talking   John
I said that was years ago   no no
no said Elsa   No said John   oh
shut up both of you   I said
they're gone

All the old women came out in the sun
and I was one

all the old gentlemen came out too
and I saw you

what a relief I said to my friend
there is no end

that's true for some but don't be so vain
he may not be the same

perhaps he's only become quite shy
one of us may die
without saying goodbye

my friend said face it that's how it goes one by one
till there's no one left on this bench in the sun

D E T O U R

I had put my days behind me
almost as they happened   rolling
faces streets personal dramas
into a scroll   quickly
quickly   sometimes my heels
were caught in the last conver-
sation   so shaking to free
myself   all that clutter flew
up into the air   scrambled
sentences my sister's death   the
name of what's his name   his mouth
his fingers   a heavy chunk of a
principled political statement
whose?

future was my intention   but
all that detritus like sand like
dust has drifted into the eyes
of my children   who after all must
continue   one of my heaviest
sorrows has just tumbled at
their feet   they stumble   what
to do   anger   fear   luckily their
children have imperiously

called offering their lives   a
detour   thank god they've all
gotten away

I had thought the tumors
on my spine would kill me but
the tumors on my head seem to be
extraordinarily competitive this week

For the past twenty or thirty years
I have eaten the freshest most
organic and colorful fruits and
vegetables   I did not drink   I
did drink one small glass of red
wine with dinner nearly every day
as suggested by *The New York Times*
I should have taken longer walks but
obviously I have done something wrong

I don't mean morally or ethically or
geographically   I did not live near
a nuclear graveyard or under a coal
stack   nor did I allow my children
to do so   I lived in a city no worse
than any other great and famous city   I
lived one story above a street that led
cabs and ambulances to the local hospital
that didn't seem so bad and was
often convenient

In any event I am
already old and therefore a little ashamed
to have written this poem full
of complaints against mortality which
biological fact I have been constructed for
to hand on to my children and grand-
children as I received it from my
dear mother and father and beloved
grandmother who all
ah   if I remember it
were in great pain at   leaving
and were furiously saying goodbye

———

ONE DAY

One day
one of us
will be lost
to the other

this has been
talked about but
lightly   turning
away   shyness   this
business of con-
fronting the
preference for
survival

      my mother said   the
      children are grown   we
      are both so sick   let us
      die together   my father
      replied   no no   you
      will be well   he lied

of course I
want you in the world
whether I'm in it or
not   your spirit
I probably mean

there is always
something to say   in
the end   speaking
without breath   one
of us will be lost
to the other

WINDOWS

this eighty-year-old body is
a fairly old body   what's it
doing around the house these days
checking the laundry   brooms
still work   what's for dinner

there are the windows   look   oh
beyond the river   Smarts Mountain
with the sun's help is recomposing all
its little hills   never saw it that way
before   windows   the afternoon story

Here we are now
      day is in charge of us   week
            is the nastiest warden
over whose head we look
      at each other   often
            with kindness

you're thinking   work
      year!   long-winded enemy
            death's timer
your mark is on me   with
      luck you'll end
            before I do

not too far away I
      blunder among hours
            exhausting the merits
                  of indolence
somehow   the story of life
      is decanted   slowly
            all my life long

—

EVEN

Even at pain's deafening intrusion
my friend could not forget the pleasant
blasphemous joking of our daily conver-
sations   she said   grace don't take me out
of the telephone book of your heart   and I
have not there she is under S for Syb   and
Claiborne still under C

SISTERS

My friends are dying
well we're old   it's natural
one day we passed the experience of "older"
which began in late middle age
and came suddenly upon "old"   then
all the little killing bugs and
baby tumors that had struggled
for years against the body's
brave immunities found their
level playing fields and
victory

but this is not what I meant to
tell you   I wanted to say that
my friends were dying but have now
become absent   the word dead is correct
but inappropriate

I have not taken their names out of
conversation   gossip   political argument
my telephone book or card index in
whatever alphabetical or contextual
organizer   I can stop any evening of
the lonesome week at Claiborne   Bercovici
Vernarelli   Deming and rest a moment

on their seriousness as artists   workers
their excitement as political actors in the
streets of our cities or in their workplaces
the vigiling   fasting   praying in or out
of jail   their lightheartedness which floated
above the year's despair
their courageous sometimes hilarious
disobediences before the state's official
servants   their fidelity to the idea that
it is possible with only a little extra anguish
to live in this world   at an absolute minimum
loving brainy sexual energetic redeemed

MABEL

Mabel   please start all over again
why go to Nova Scotia
when you live in Maine
why take the coal mine trail
don't you know you're a
useful person   one of the
five or six in this world

You can't guess that you have
done more good than any of us do-
gooders even when impeded by
George's brains   girls   gardens

Mabel I don't know how to write this
poem which is after all a love poem
only about the way we often
looked at each other with something
like the plain pleasure of two women who
have guessed what it was all about
and wished they'd lived next door
for at least ten or fifteen years
maybe somewhere within a fifty-mile radius of each other
on a fast road

EDUCATION

To have lived long enough
and not too far from the dying
of a couple of ancient trees
the high leaf and flowering
above broken arms   to have known
one great tree full and sturdy
then in my own years
the arbitrary swords of sunscald
lightning   scar   scab   rot

in the woods behind our house
uprooted storm-thrown hemlock
(hurricane of 'thirty-eight) a humped
and heaving graveyard   do you see that

it's good in one ordinary life
to have witnessed the hard labor
of a long death   the way one
high branch can still advance alone   pale green
and greener   into the sun's
nutritious light

LET THE DAY GO

      who needs it
I had another day in mind
something like this one
      sunny green   the earth
just right   having suffered
the assault of what is called
torrential rain   the pepper
the basil   sitting upright
in their little boxes waiting
I suppose for me   also the
cosmos   the zinnias nearly
blooming   a year too late
forget it   let the day go
the sweet green day   let it
take care of itself

T H I S H I L L

this hill
crossed with broken pines and maples
lumpy with the burial mounds
of uprooted hemlocks (hurricane
of 'thirty-eight)   out of their rotting hearts
generations rise trying once more
to become the forest

just beyond them
tall enough to be called trees
in their youth like aspen   a bouquet
of young beech is gathered

they still wear last summer's leaves
the lightest brown almost translucent
how their stubbornness decorates
the winter woods

on this narrow path
ice holds the black undecaying
oak leaves in its crackling grip
oh   it's become too hard to walk
        a sunny patch   I'm suddenly
in water to my ankles   April